Where Would I Be Without You, *Mom?*
A Loving Treasury of Cherished Memories
R.J. Fischer

PINNACLE BOOKS
http://www.pinnaclebooks.com

PINNACLE BOOKS are published by

Kensington Publishing Corp.
850 Third Avenue
New York, NY 10022

Copyright © 1998 by Joanne Fluke and Ruel Fischmann

All rights reserved. No part of this book may be reproduced in any form or by any means without the prior written consent of the Publisher, excepting brief quotes used in reviews.

If you purchased this book without a cover, you should be aware that this book is stolen property. It was reported as "unsold and destroyed" to the Publisher and neither the Author nor the Publisher has received any payment for this "stripped book."

Pinnacle and the P logo Reg. U.S. Pat. & TM Off.

First Printing: May, 1998
10 9 8 7 6 5 4 3 2 1

Printed in the United States of America

Lois & Neal,
Hope you
enjoy this!
Joanne

This book is dedicated to Jami
who's a great candidate for Super Mom

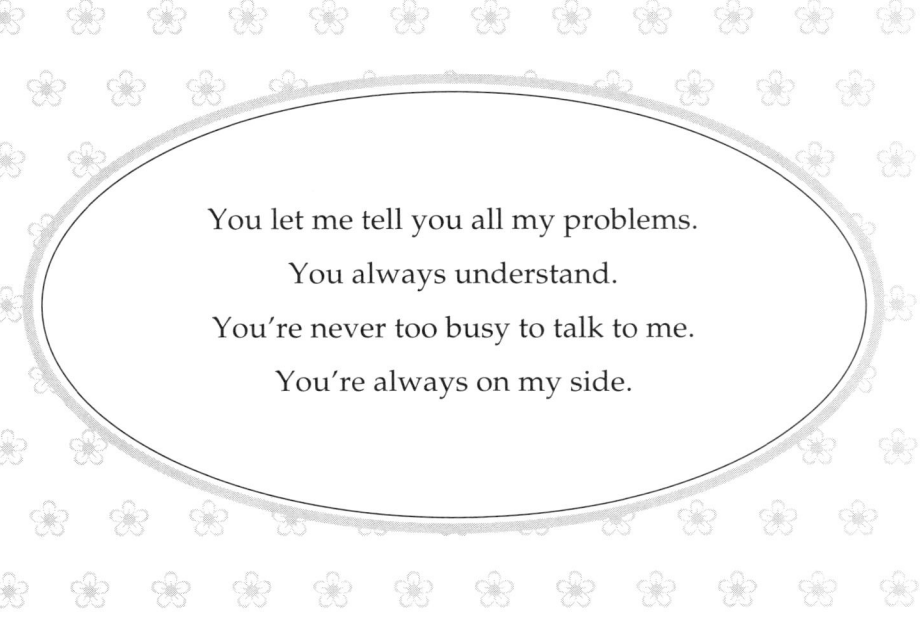

You let me tell you all my problems.

You always understand.

You're never too busy to talk to me.

You're always on my side.

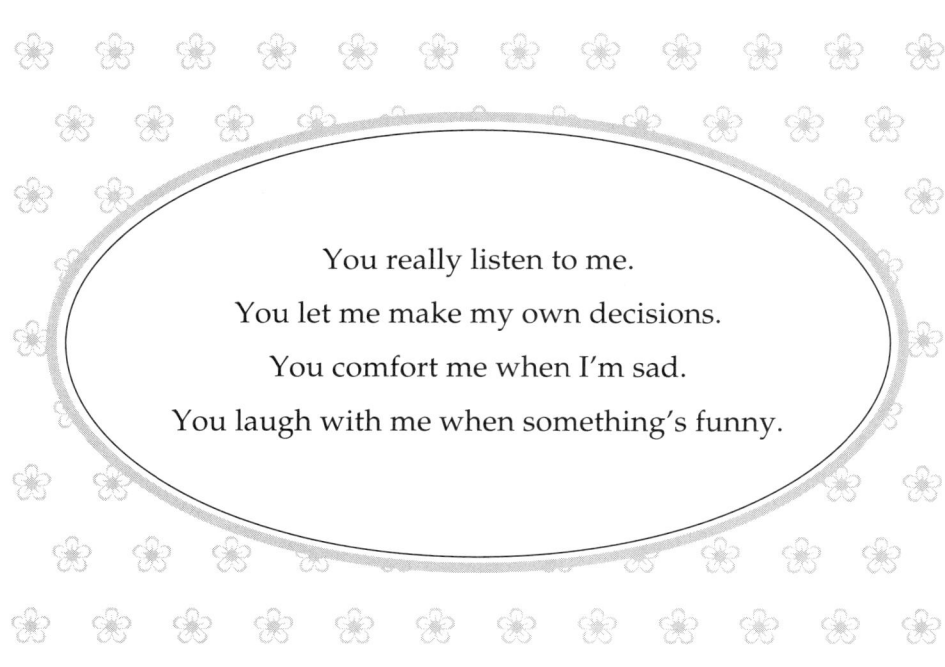

You really listen to me.
You let me make my own decisions.
You comfort me when I'm sad.
You laugh with me when something's funny.

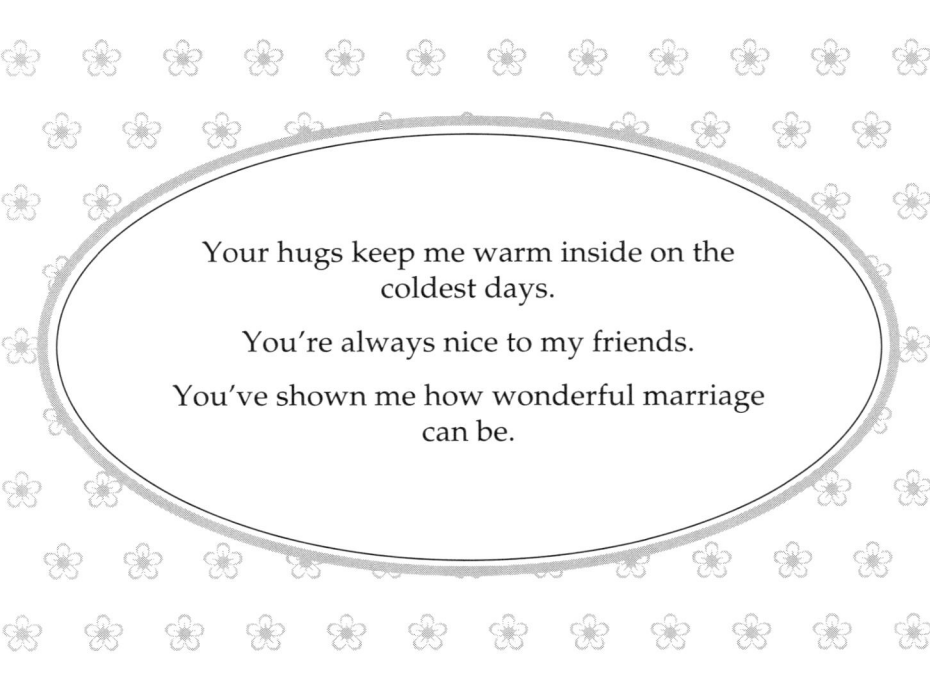

Your hugs keep me warm inside on the coldest days.

You're always nice to my friends.

You've shown me how wonderful marriage can be.

You framed the first picture I drew for you and hung it on the wall.

You kept me from being too nervous on my first date.

Even if I move far away, your love will always be in my heart.

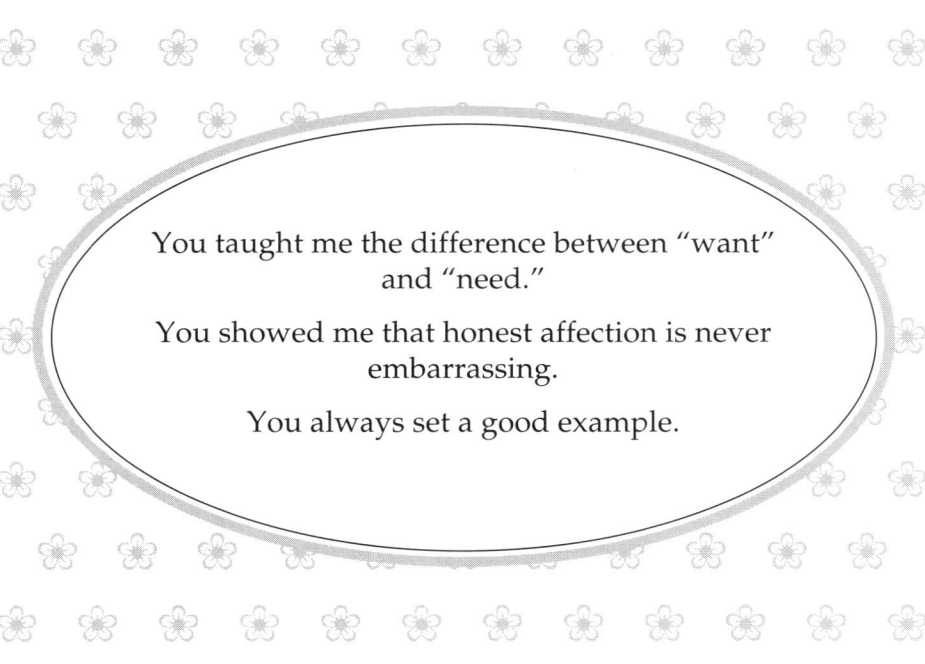

You taught me the difference between "want" and "need."

You showed me that honest affection is never embarrassing.

You always set a good example.

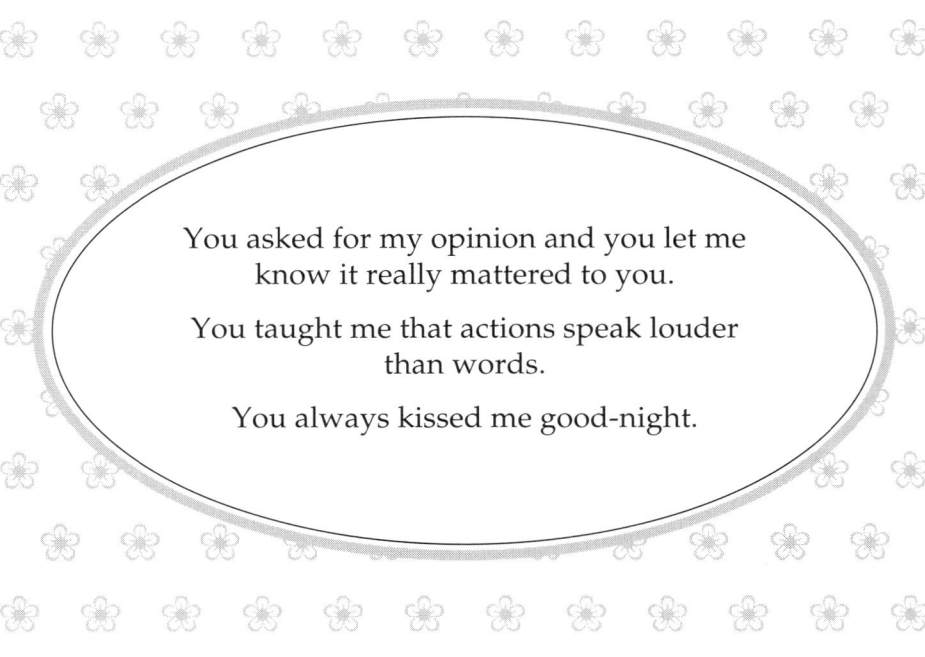

You asked for my opinion and you let me know it really mattered to you.

You taught me that actions speak louder than words.

You always kissed me good-night.

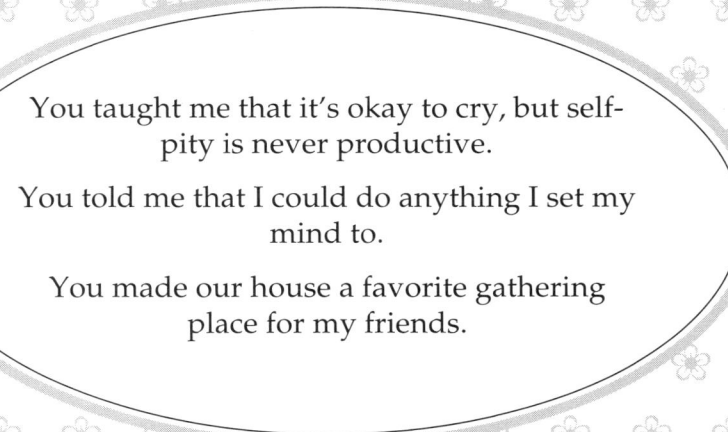

You taught me that it's okay to cry, but self-pity is never productive.

You told me that I could do anything I set my mind to.

You made our house a favorite gathering place for my friends.

You always told my friends it was no trouble to set an extra place at the table.

Instead of yelling at my mistakes, you just asked me what we could do to fix them.

You taught me to appreciate all music, not just "my kind."

You taught me that there's always more than one way of doing things.

You let me make small mistakes so that I'd learn to avoid the big ones.

You taught me to be tolerant of other people's opinions, even when I didn't agree with them.

You made home a safe place to be.

You taught me that words can be weapons
and I should think before I speak.

You taught me that people are a great resource
and all I have to do is seek them out.

You taught me that nothing is too difficult for someone who is eager to learn.

You showed me that the best compliment is one that comes from the heart.

You taught me to take little disappointments in stride.

You showed me how to weigh the pros and cons in my mind before I made a decision.

You took walks with me and taught me to really see the world around me.

You taught me that a friendly smile makes a great first impression.

You taught me that guilt feels awful, but it can be avoided by thinking before I act.

You taught me that failure is not the end of the world.

You taught me that by bringing joy to someone else's life, I bring joy to my own.

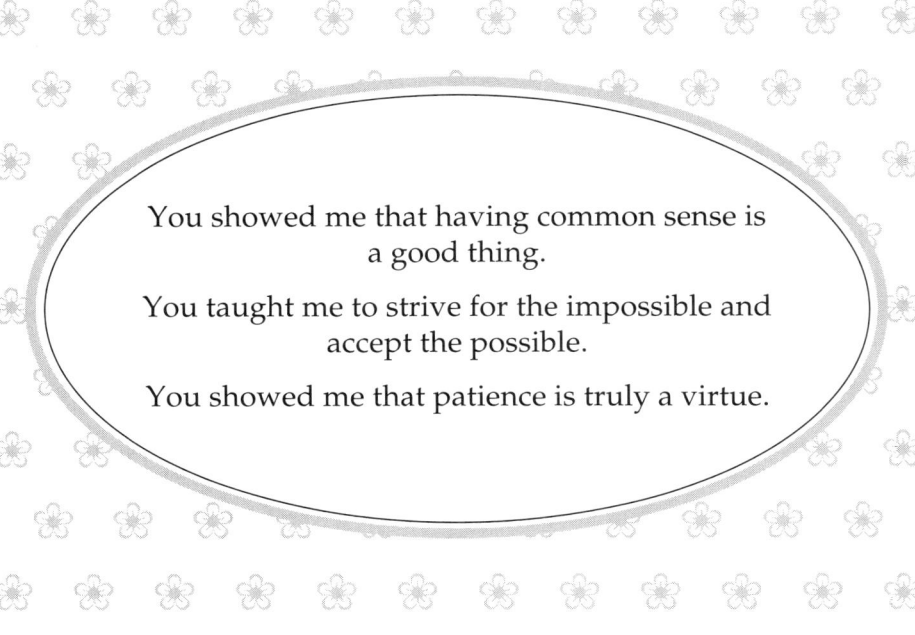

You showed me that having common sense is a good thing.

You taught me to strive for the impossible and accept the possible.

You showed me that patience is truly a virtue.

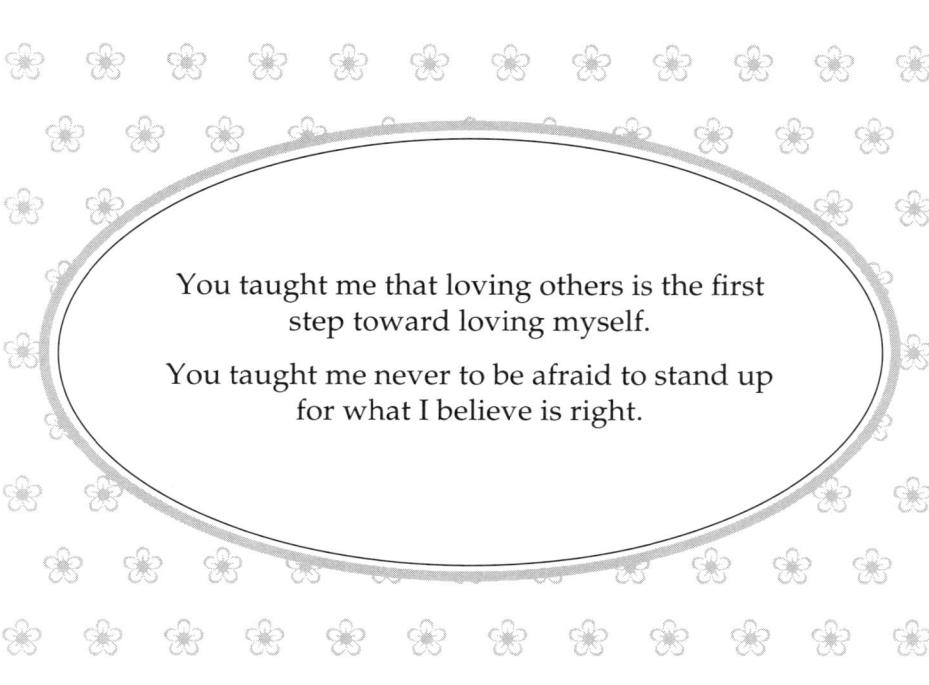

You taught me that loving others is the first step toward loving myself.

You taught me never to be afraid to stand up for what I believe is right.

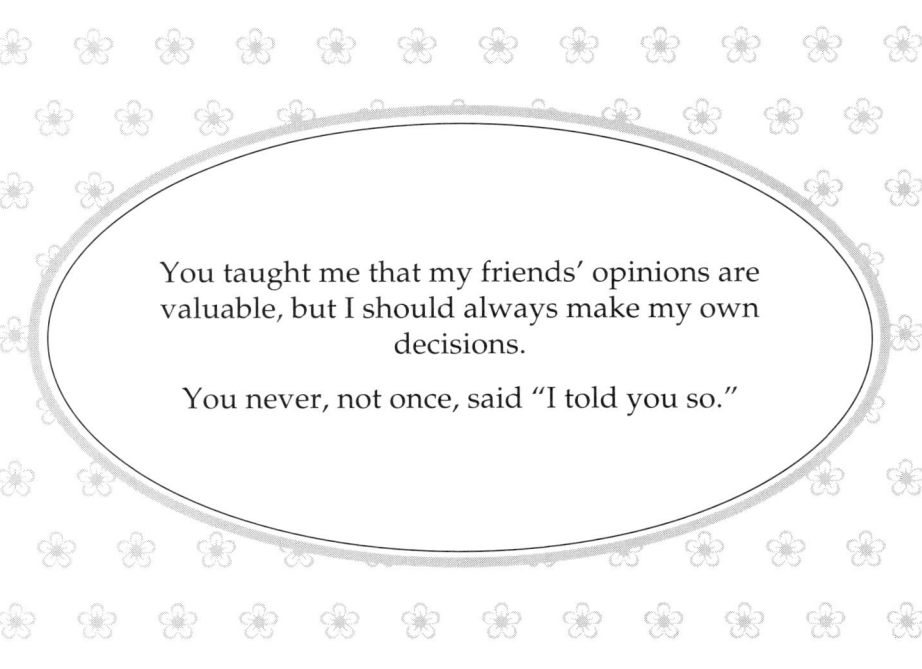

You taught me that my friends' opinions are valuable, but I should always make my own decisions.

You never, not once, said "I told you so."

Instead of saying "I wish you hadn't . . ." you always said, "Okay, where do we go from here?"

You knew there were some things I couldn't change and you showed me how to cope with them.

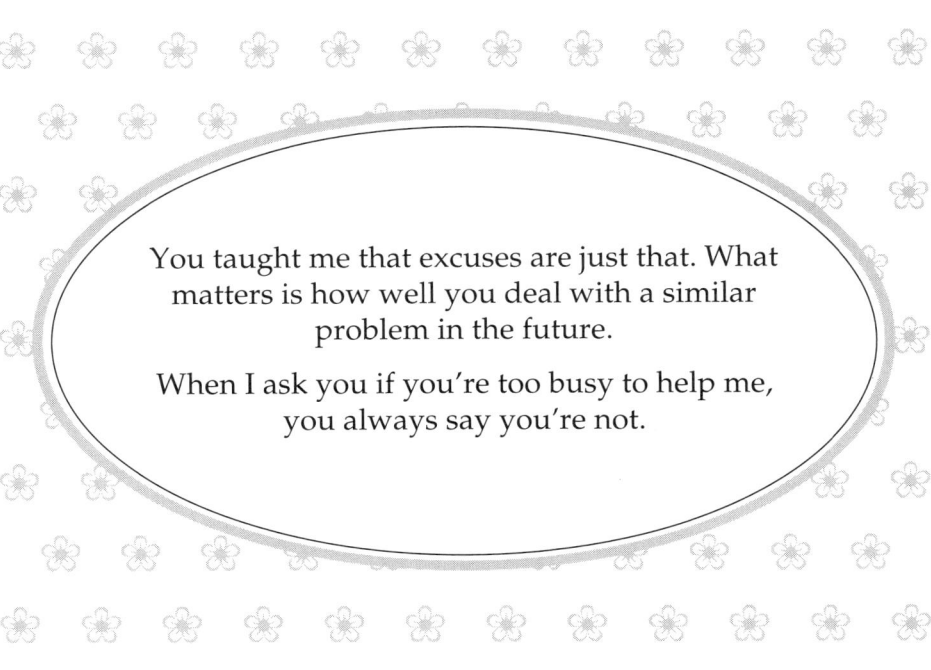

You taught me that excuses are just that. What matters is how well you deal with a similar problem in the future.

When I ask you if you're too busy to help me, you always say you're not.

You always have a smile, especially when I need one the most.

You taught me that love comes in all shapes and sizes.

You taught me that sometimes it's necessary to say "no."

You gave me an allowance when I was young and taught me how to budget my money.

You never got mad at me, only at what I did.

You had a silly, pet name for me, but you never used it in front of my friends.

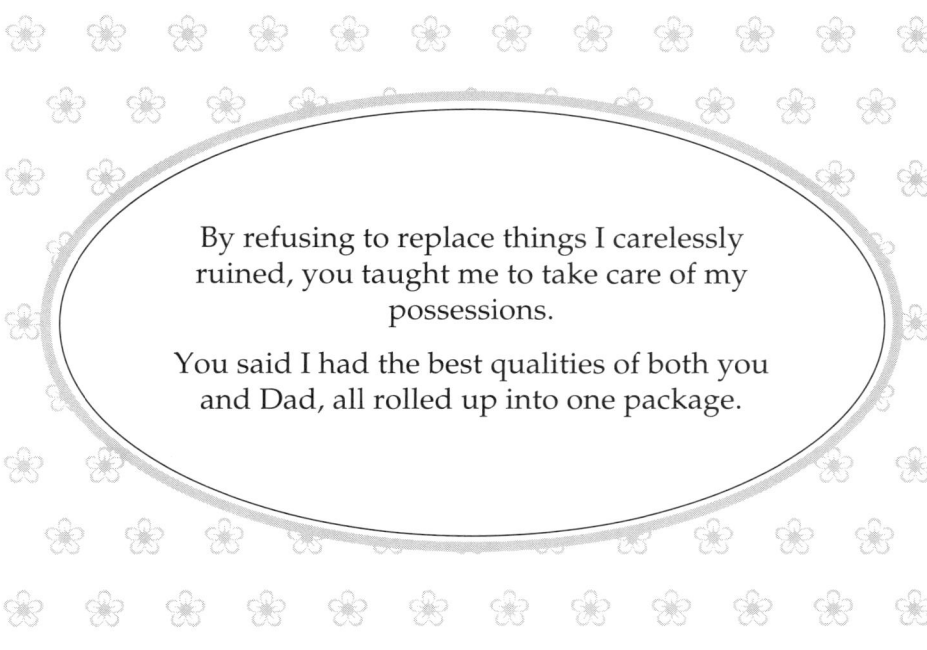

By refusing to replace things I carelessly ruined, you taught me to take care of my possessions.

You said I had the best qualities of both you and Dad, all rolled up into one package.

You let me lock the door to my room so it was my private place.

You taught me that putting off things until the last minute just makes them harder to do.

You read to me and when I learned to read, you let me read to you.

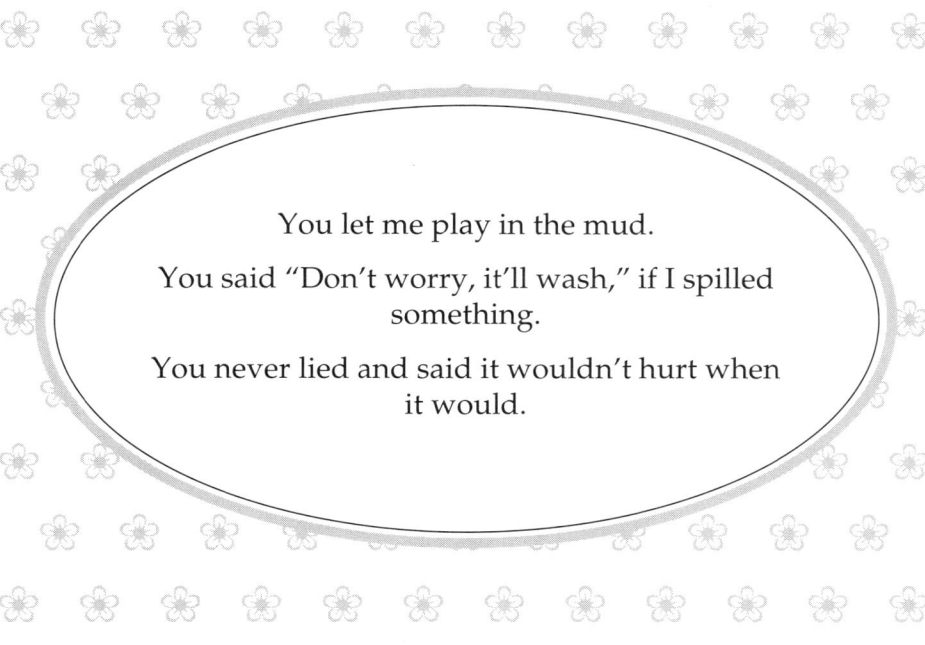

You let me play in the mud.

You said "Don't worry, it'll wash," if I spilled something.

You never lied and said it wouldn't hurt when it would.

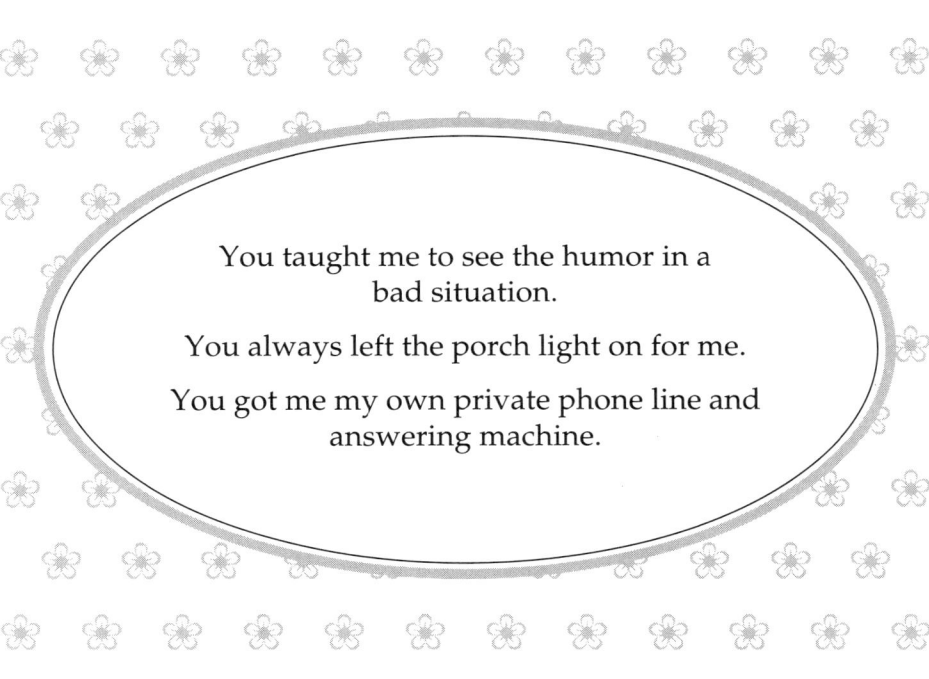

You taught me to see the humor in a bad situation.

You always left the porch light on for me.

You got me my own private phone line and answering machine.

You never made me leave the room when you discussed a problem with Dad.

You refused to repeat anything I told you in confidence.

You made family dinners fun.

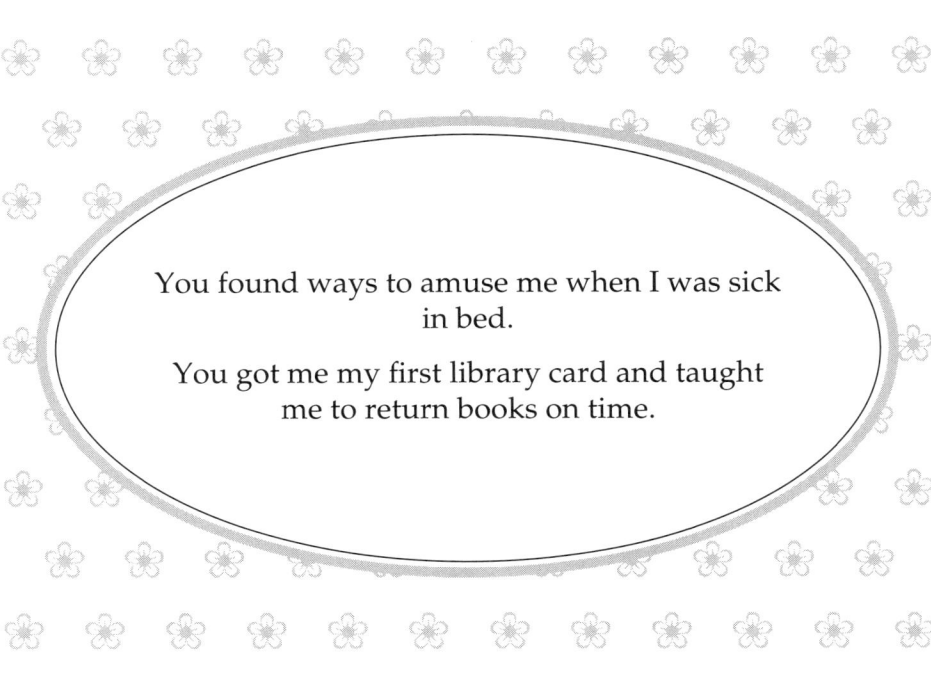

You found ways to amuse me when I was sick in bed.

You got me my first library card and taught me to return books on time.

When I picked dandelions for you, you put them on the dining room table in your best vase.

You let my puppy sleep in bed with me.

You let me borrow your car when mine was in the shop.

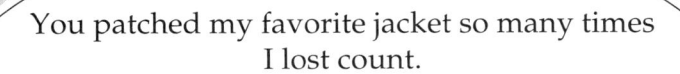

You patched my favorite jacket so many times
I lost count.

You had "junk food night" once a month and
you let us eat anything we wanted.

You always had a Band-Aid ready for
my owies.

You taught me that a combination of chicken soup and love is the best cure for a cold.

You treated my little problems with the same seriousness as my big problems.

You're never too busy to baby-sit with the grandkids.

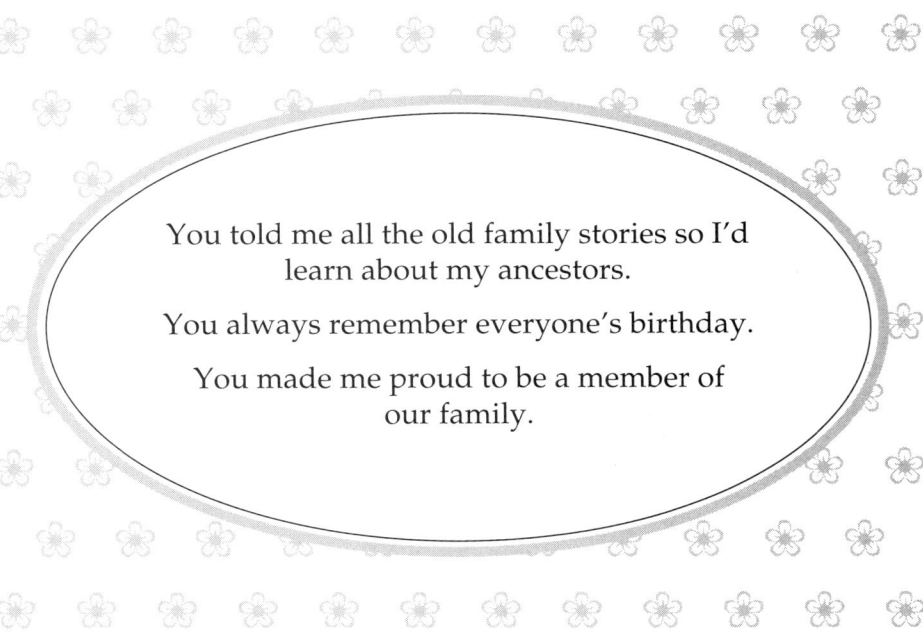

You told me all the old family stories so I'd learn about my ancestors.

You always remember everyone's birthday.

You made me proud to be a member of our family.

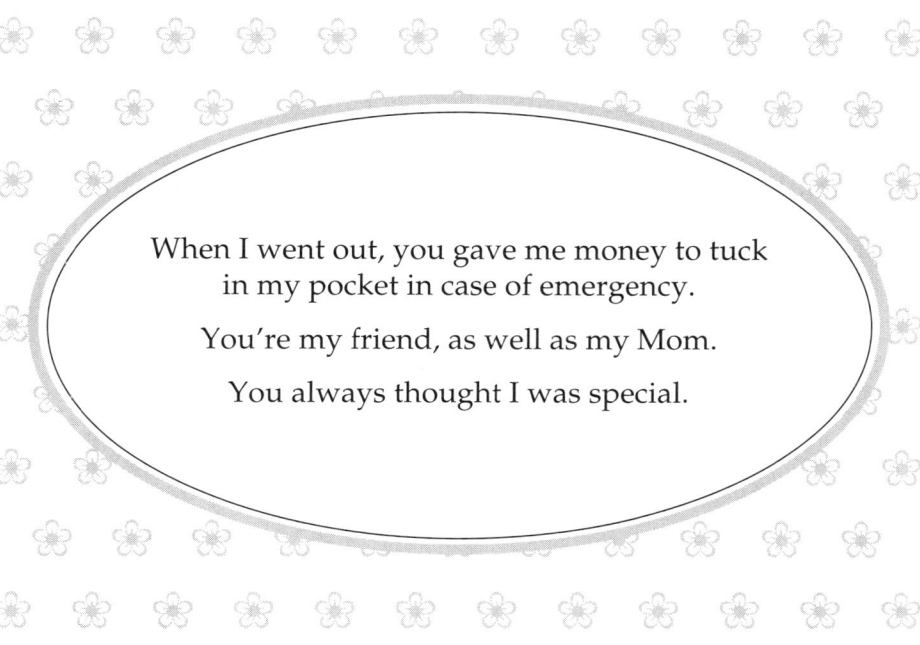

When I went out, you gave me money to tuck in my pocket in case of emergency.

You're my friend, as well as my Mom.

You always thought I was special.

You taught me that it's better to be safe than sorry.

When I felt threatened, I knew you'd protect me.

You taught me that there's nothing so enjoyable as a good book on a rainy afternoon.

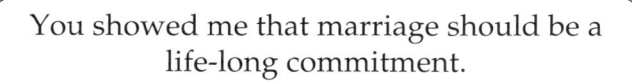

You showed me that marriage should be a life-long commitment.

You taught me never to say anything on the phone that I wouldn't say face-to-face.

You taught me that not everyone is going to love me.

You kept the family traditions alive.

You let me help you trim the Christmas tree, even when I was too little to reach anything but the bottom branches.

You taught me never to give up.

You taught me to respect other people's religions.

You showed me that the best cure for loneliness is to keep busy.

After you made frosting, you let me lick the bowl.

You made my friends feel that you were their friend, too.

You said that hand-me-downs were like gifts from one member of the family to another.

You taught me never to throw anything away if it could be given to charity.

You taught me to live each day to the fullest.

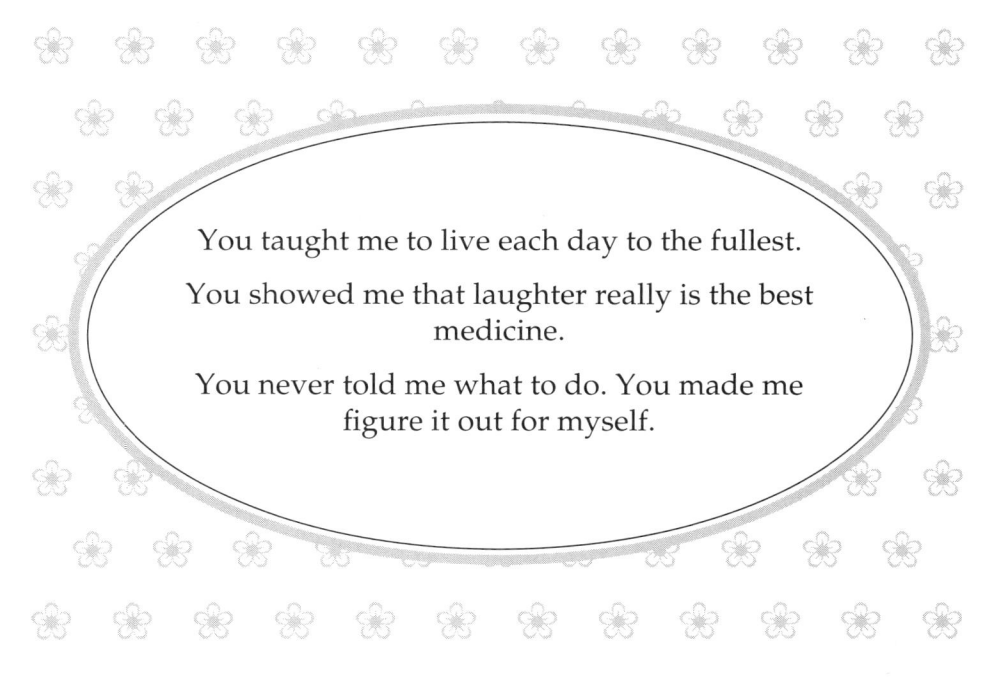

You showed me that laughter really is the best medicine.

You never told me what to do. You made me figure it out for myself.

You let me be a kid.

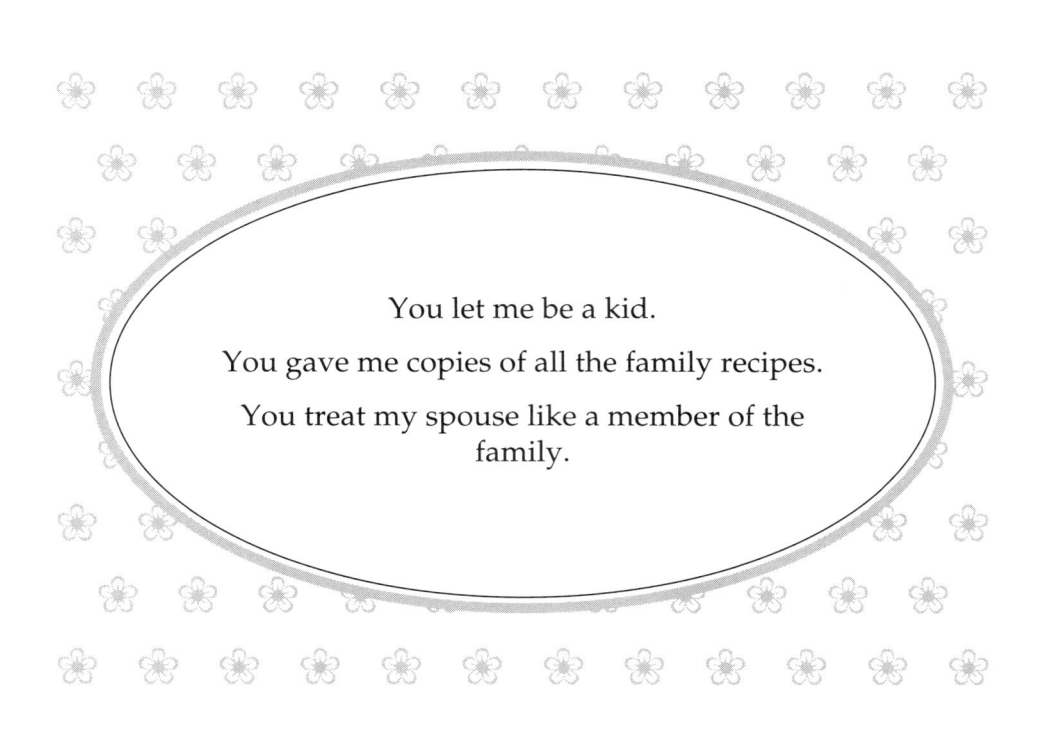

You gave me copies of all the family recipes.

You treat my spouse like a member of the family.

You never laughed at me, unless I was deliberately trying to be funny.

You let me get contact lenses when I thought glasses looked ugly on me.

You taught me that if I belittled others, I also belittled myself.

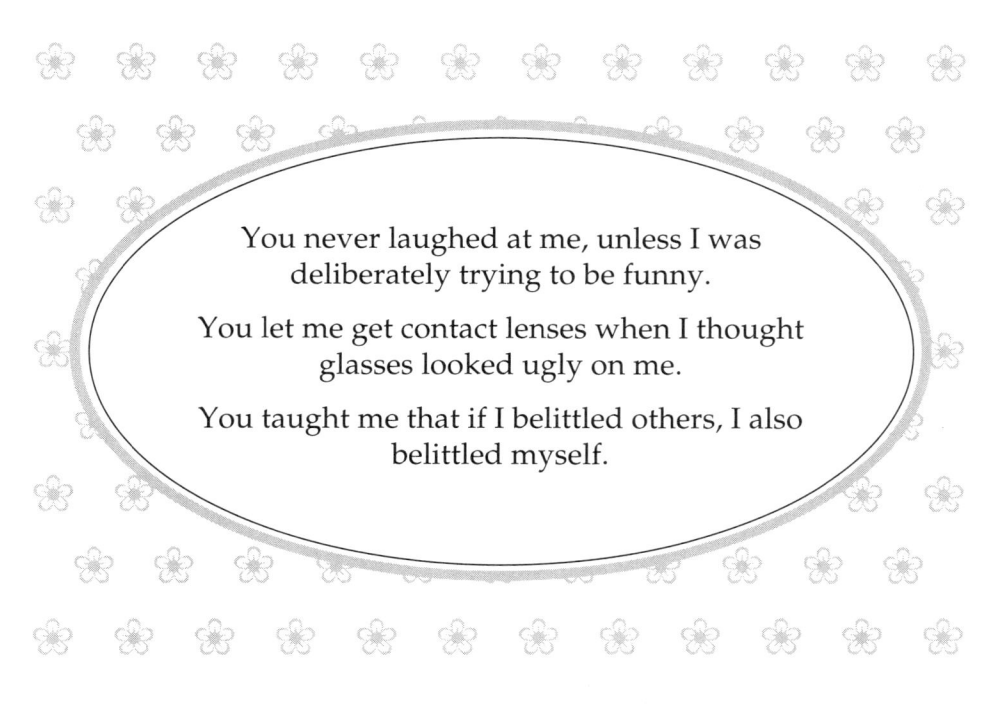

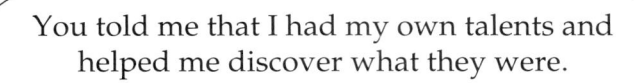

You told me that I had my own talents and helped me discover what they were.

You were always glad to see me when I came home.

You set limits and made sure I understood them.

You proved to me that it's easier to find things in a clean room.

You agreed to change a rule if I could give you a good reason to do so.

You taught me that everything had a price and I had to decide whether or not it was worth it.

You were never arbitrary.

You taught me that when I'm not sure what to wear, something basic is always acceptable.

The house never smelled as good as when you were baking chocolate chip cookies.

You never let me get away with lying to you.

You taught me that kindness always comes back around.

You were my safety net when I tested my wings.

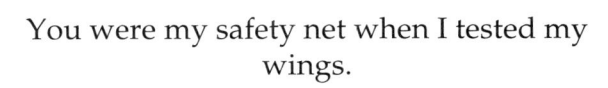

You trusted my judgment.

You taught me about birth control.

You always made sure I got a good breakfast.

You showed me that no one is ever too old to play a children's game.

You showed me how much fun it was to do things as a family.

You taught me that clean-up is necessary and it goes much faster if everyone pitches in to help.

You kept a scrapbook, just for me.

You never got mad when my friends raided our refrigerator.

I knew I could always call you collect.

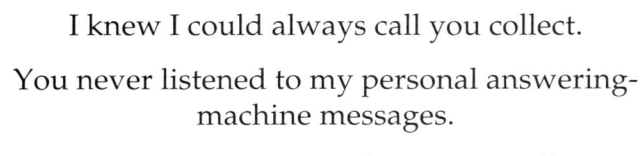

You never listened to my personal answering-machine messages.

You taught me never to let anyone talk me into something I knew I shouldn't do.

You taught me to imagine what it would be like to be in somebody else's shoes.

You encouraged me to be creative, even when it didn't turn out exactly right.

You proved that long car trips can be fun if you keep your eyes open for new things.

You taught me how to pack a suitcase so my clothes wouldn't wrinkle.

You taught me that depression lasts only as long as you let it.

You taught me that words spoken in anger can never be unsaid.

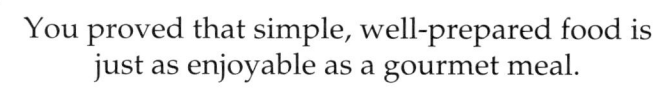

You proved that simple, well-prepared food is just as enjoyable as a gourmet meal.

You made me admit it when I was wrong and showed me how to correct my mistakes.

You let me play in the sprinklers.

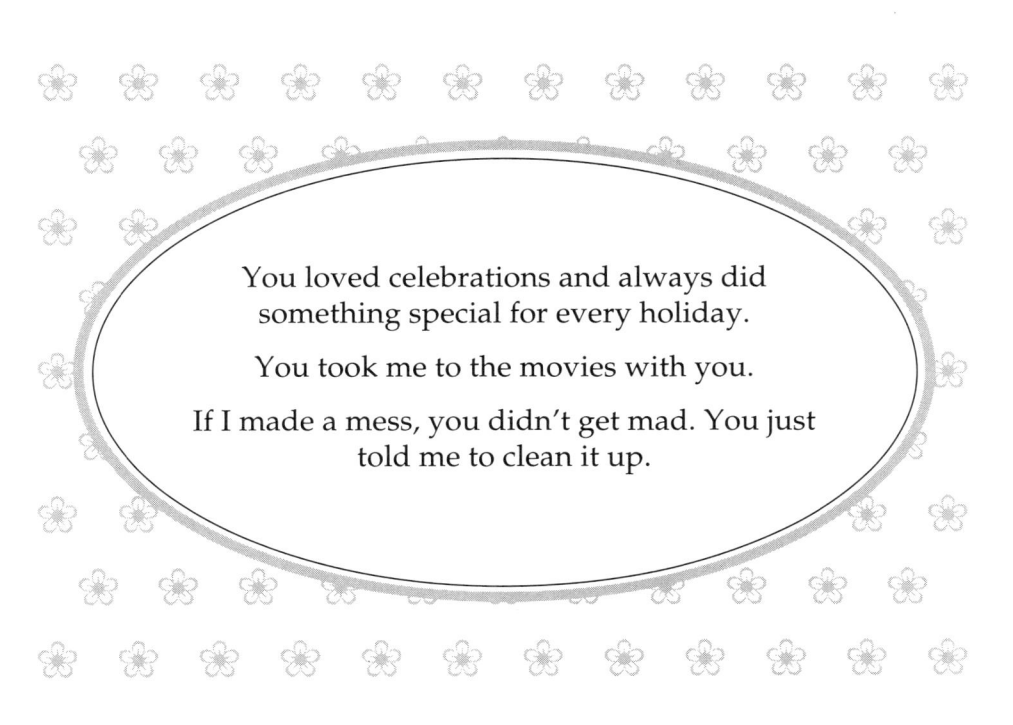

You loved celebrations and always did something special for every holiday.

You took me to the movies with you.

If I made a mess, you didn't get mad. You just told me to clean it up.

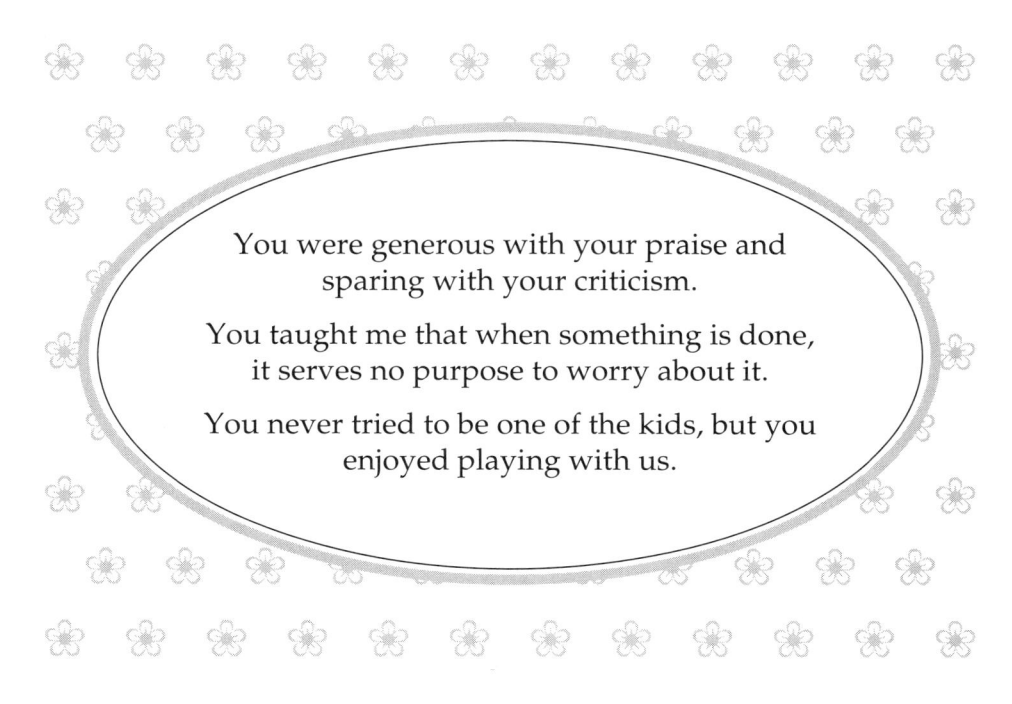

You were generous with your praise and sparing with your criticism.

You taught me that when something is done, it serves no purpose to worry about it.

You never tried to be one of the kids, but you enjoyed playing with us.

You never sent me off to school without a hug.

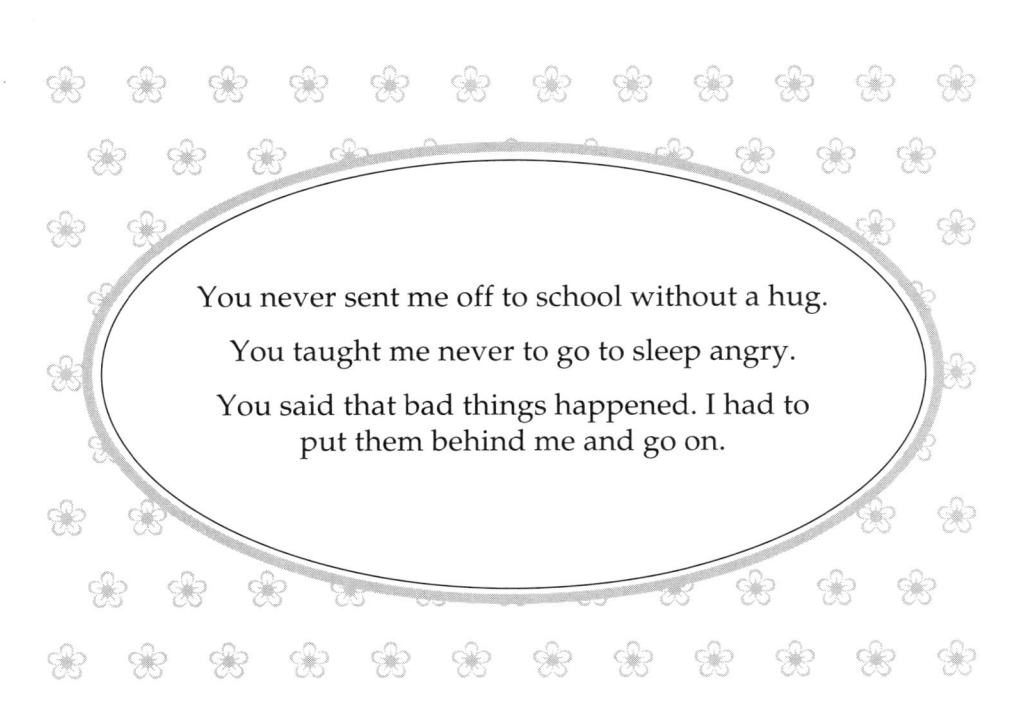

You taught me never to go to sleep angry.

You said that bad things happened. I had to put them behind me and go on.

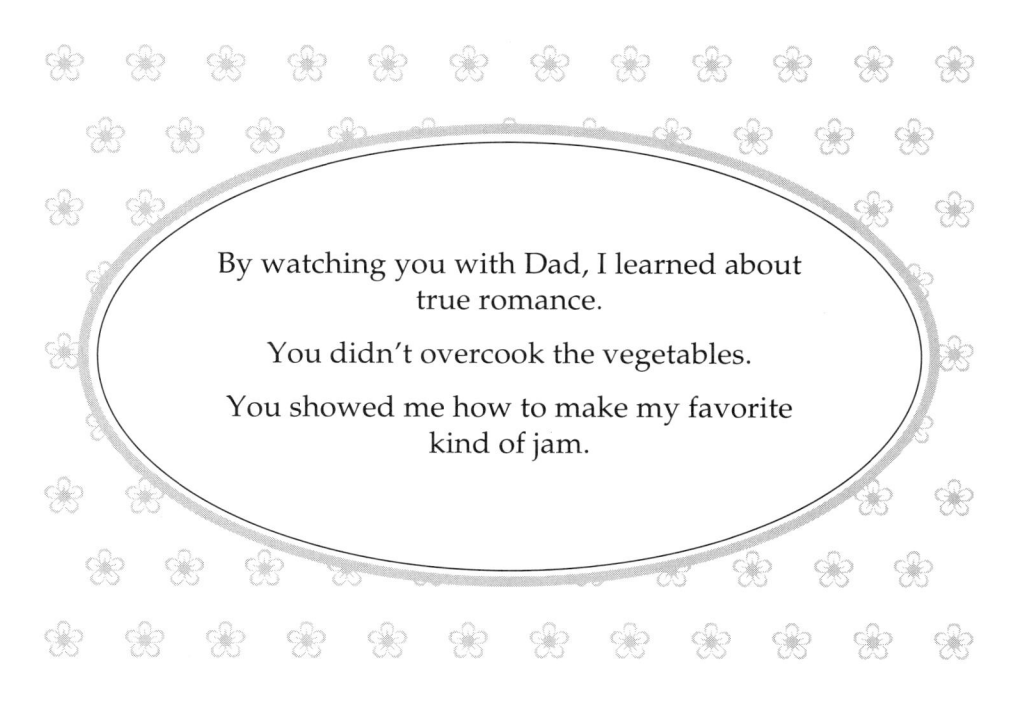

By watching you with Dad, I learned about true romance.

You didn't overcook the vegetables.

You showed me how to make my favorite kind of jam.

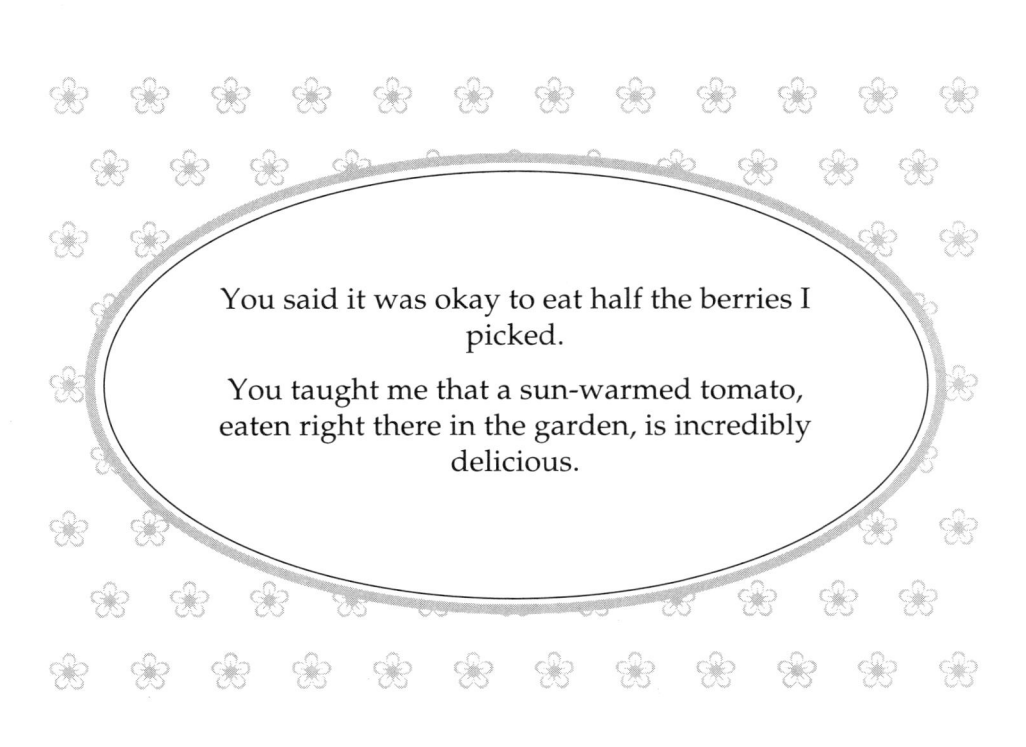

You said it was okay to eat half the berries I picked.

You taught me that a sun-warmed tomato, eaten right there in the garden, is incredibly delicious.

You taught me to blow the fluff off a dandelion.

The Halloween costumes you made for me were the envy of all my friends.

You displayed every award I ever won in school.

You let me decorate the Christmas cookies and said they were beautiful.

You dressed up in a costume and took me trick-or-treating when I was too young to go by myself.

You helped me make a snowman.

When I was too little to go down the big slide, you let me ride down on your lap.

When it rained, you let me set up my tent in the living room and pretend I was camping in the woods.

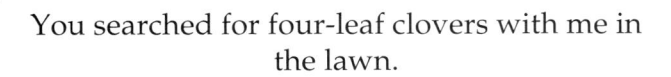

You searched for four-leaf clovers with me in the lawn.

You taught me that a secret might not stay a secret if you tell it to someone.

You taught me never to believe in gossip.

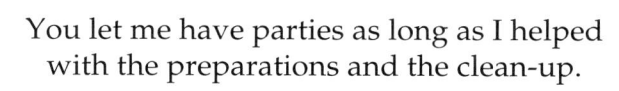

You let me have parties as long as I helped with the preparations and the clean-up.

You taught me that the first step toward having good friends is being a good friend.

You showed me that a few moments of quiet reflection could make the rest of the day go smoother.

You made sure that none of my guests ever felt like an outsider.

When you gave me gifts, it was something I wanted, not something you wanted me to have.

You left messages on the kitchen bulletin board for me and taught me to do the same.

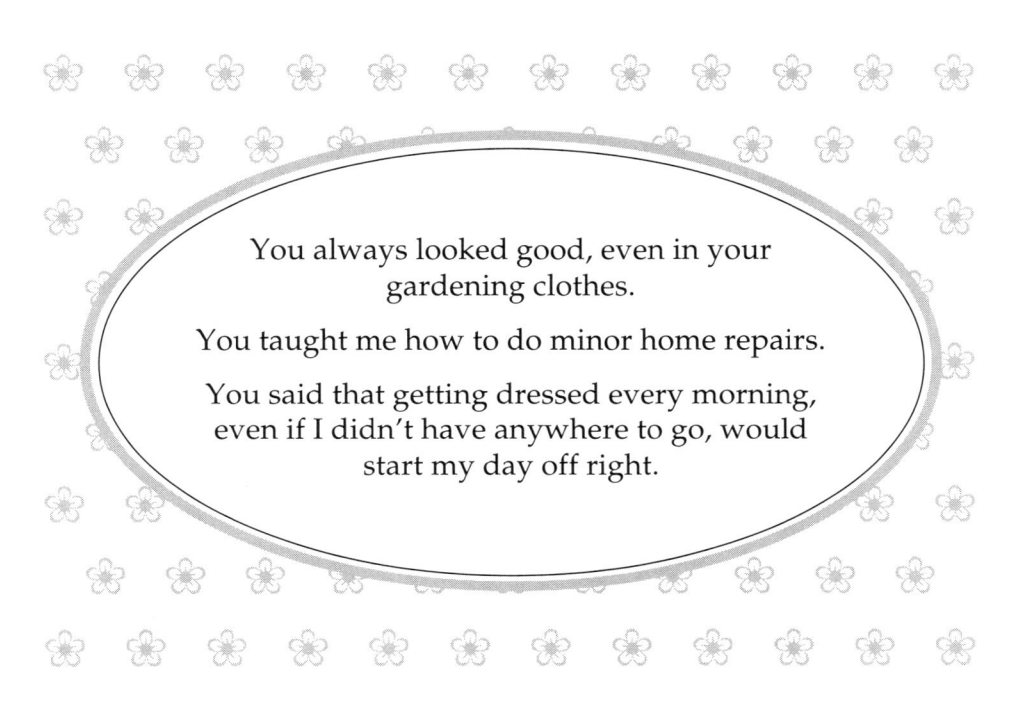

You always looked good, even in your gardening clothes.

You taught me how to do minor home repairs.

You said that getting dressed every morning, even if I didn't have anywhere to go, would start my day off right.

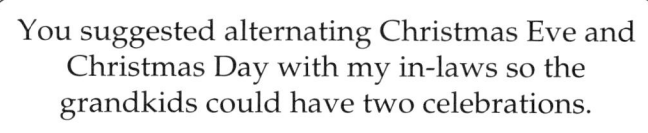

You suggested alternating Christmas Eve and Christmas Day with my in-laws so the grandkids could have two celebrations.

If one of my friends didn't have somewhere to go for a holiday, you were quick to offer an invitation.

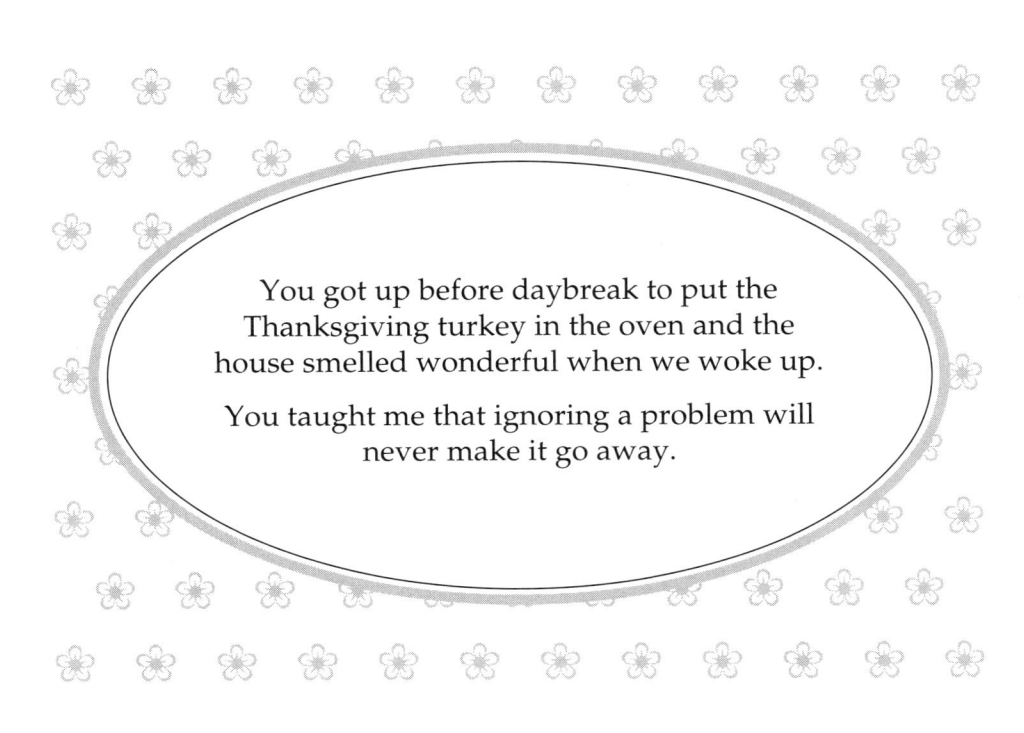

You got up before daybreak to put the Thanksgiving turkey in the oven and the house smelled wonderful when we woke up.

You taught me that ignoring a problem will never make it go away.

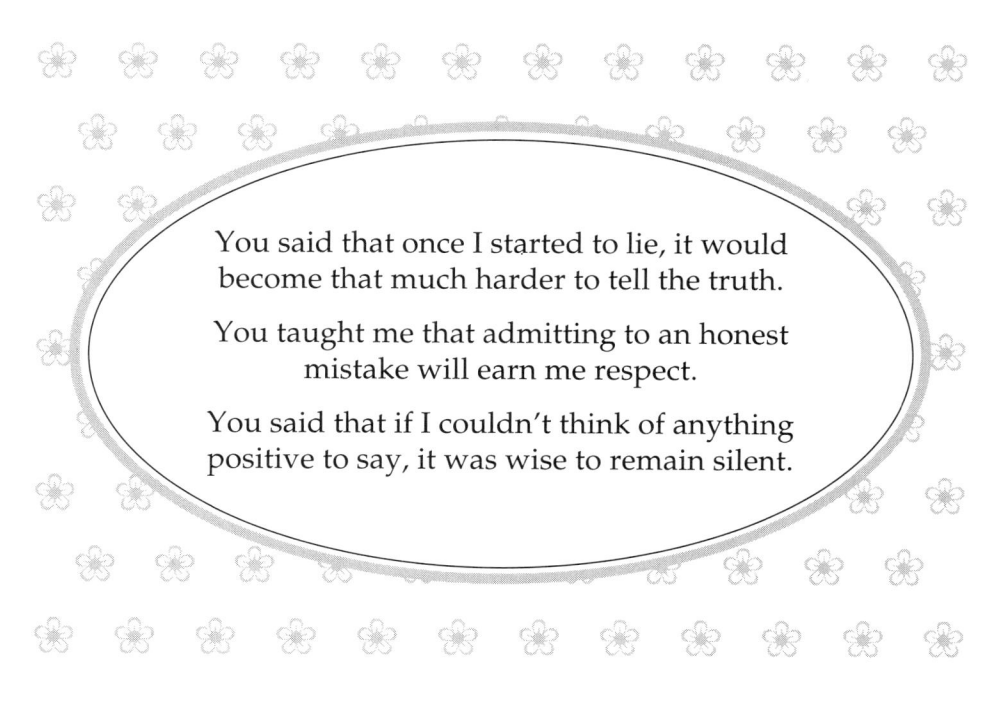

You said that once I started to lie, it would become that much harder to tell the truth.

You taught me that admitting to an honest mistake will earn me respect.

You said that if I couldn't think of anything positive to say, it was wise to remain silent.

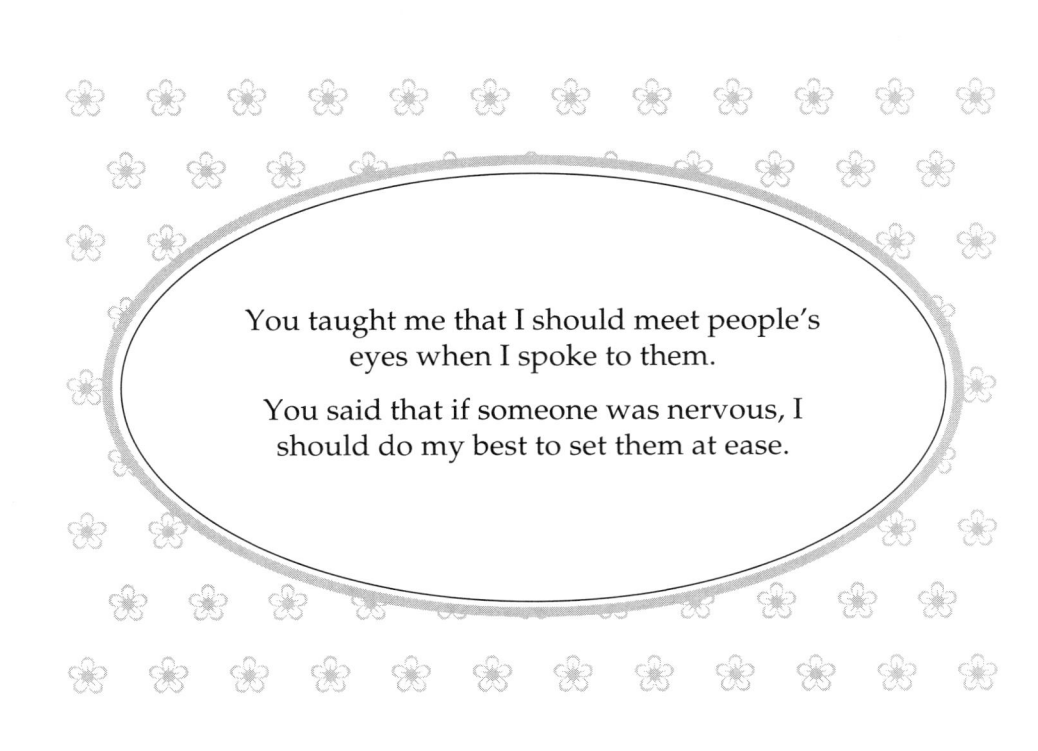

You taught me that I should meet people's eyes when I spoke to them.

You said that if someone was nervous, I should do my best to set them at ease.

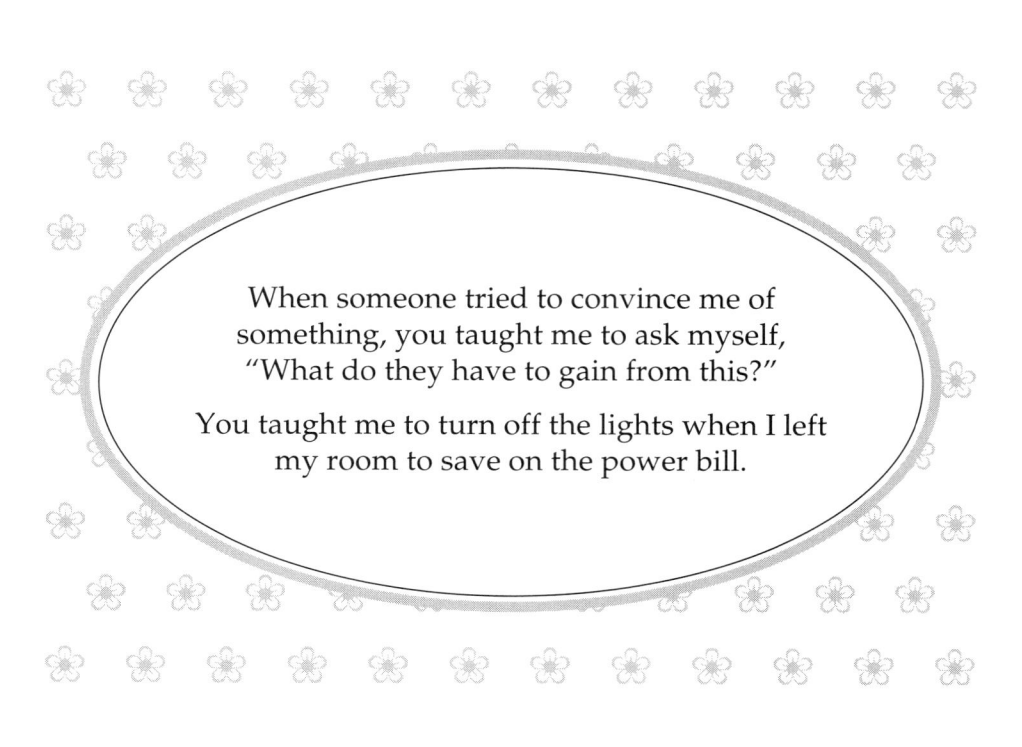

When someone tried to convince me of something, you taught me to ask myself, "What do they have to gain from this?"

You taught me to turn off the lights when I left my room to save on the power bill.

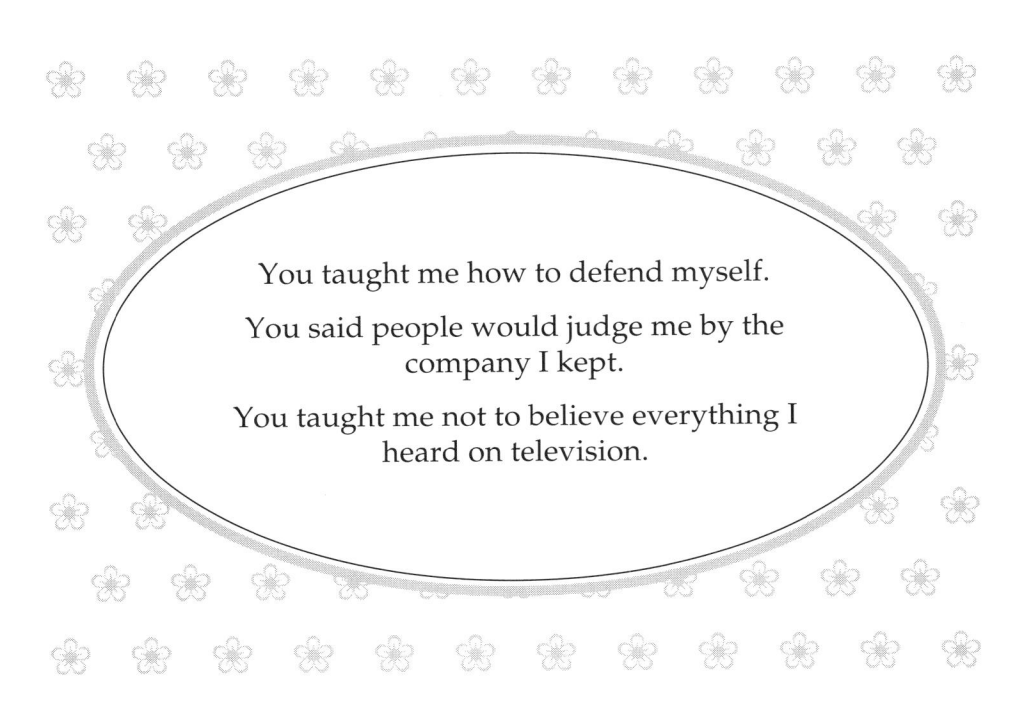

You taught me how to defend myself.

You said people would judge me by the company I kept.

You taught me not to believe everything I heard on television.

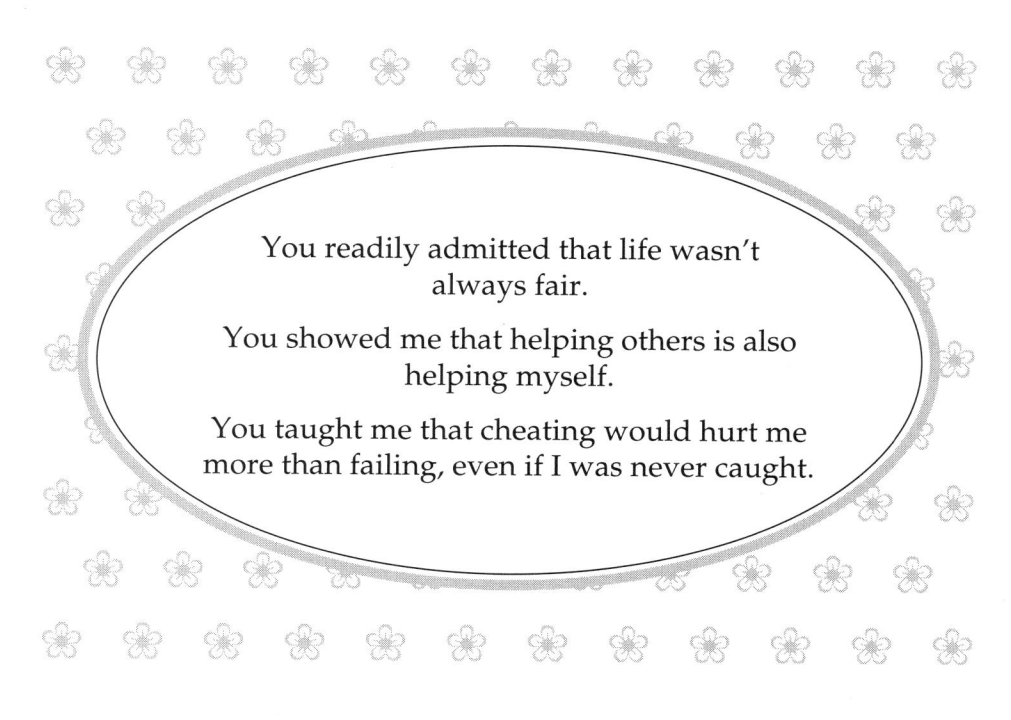

You readily admitted that life wasn't always fair.

You showed me that helping others is also helping myself.

You taught me that cheating would hurt me more than failing, even if I was never caught.

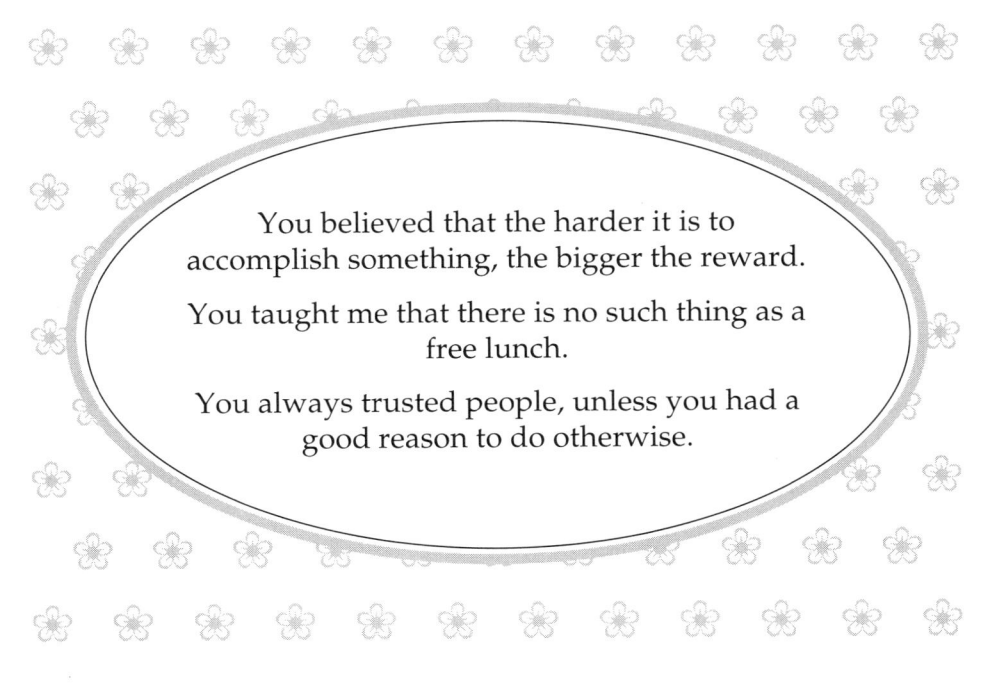

You believed that the harder it is to accomplish something, the bigger the reward.

You taught me that there is no such thing as a free lunch.

You always trusted people, unless you had a good reason to do otherwise.

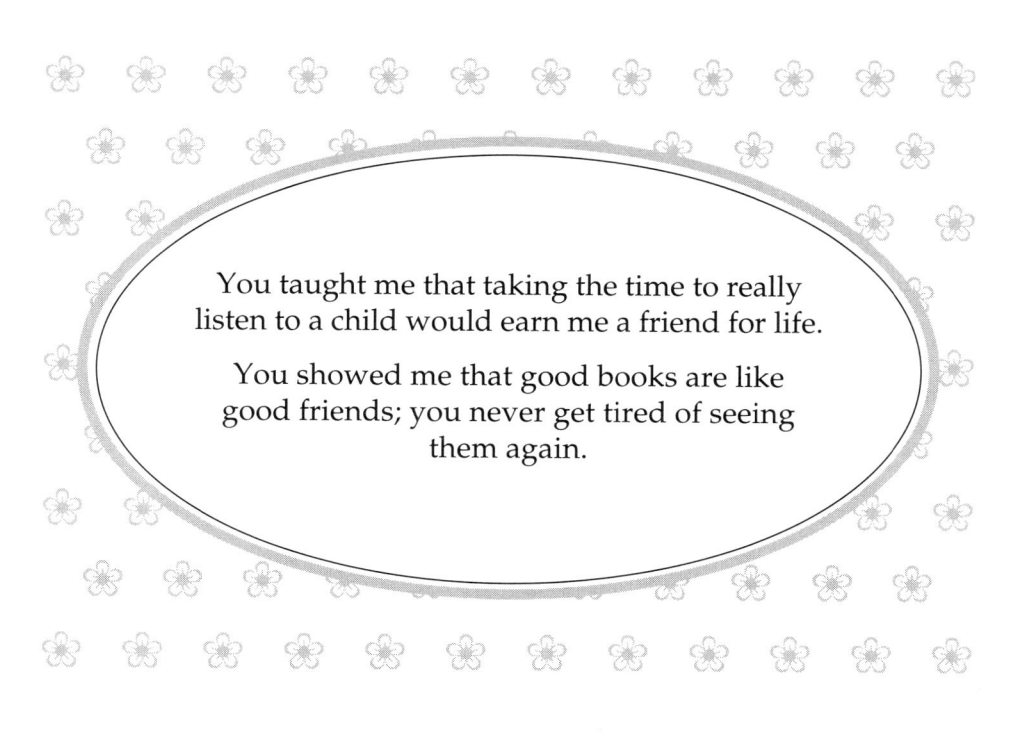

You taught me that taking the time to really listen to a child would earn me a friend for life.

You showed me that good books are like good friends; you never get tired of seeing them again.

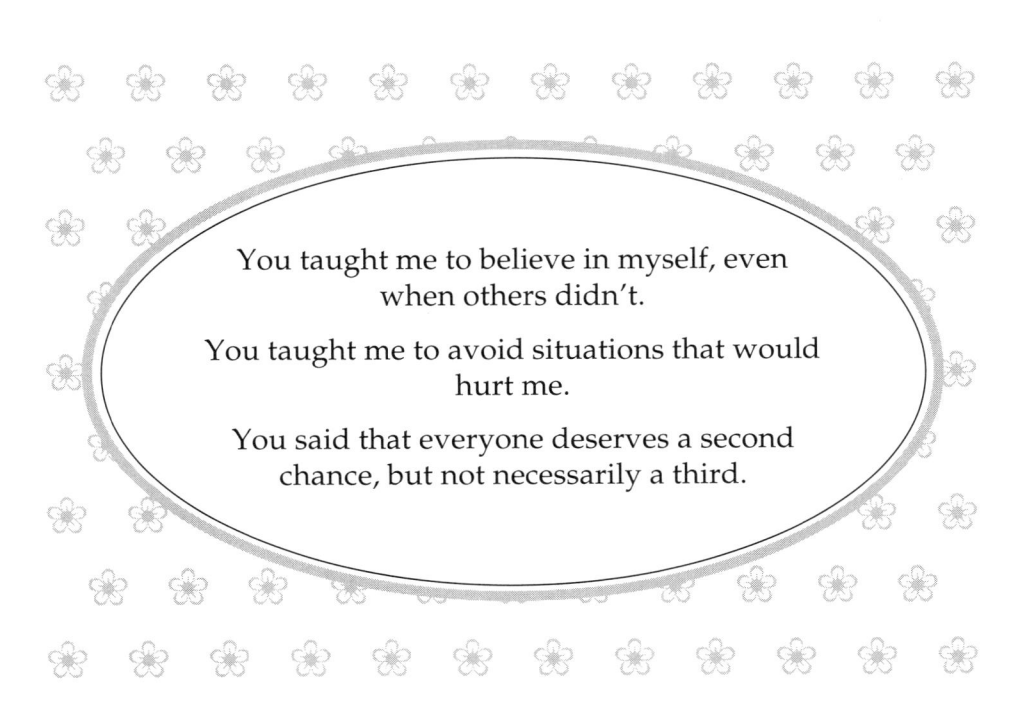

You taught me to believe in myself, even when others didn't.

You taught me to avoid situations that would hurt me.

You said that everyone deserves a second chance, but not necessarily a third.

You taught me to mean it when I said no, and not to back down without a very good reason.

You taught me to consider all my options and choose the one that was best.

You said that if my decisions were good ones, I would be able to live with them.

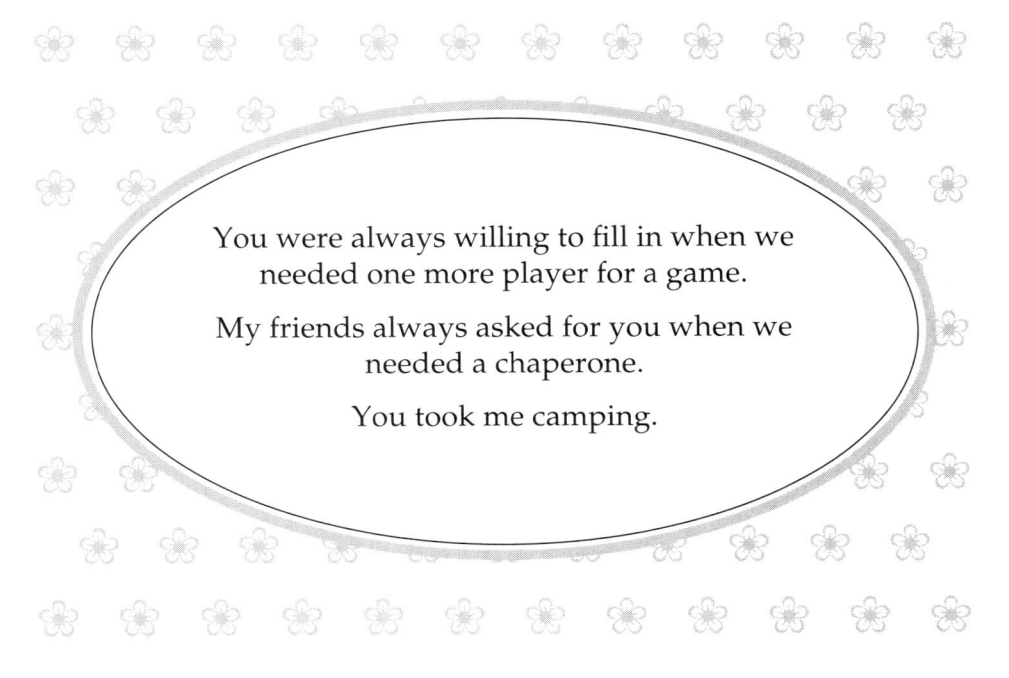

You were always willing to fill in when we needed one more player for a game.

My friends always asked for you when we needed a chaperone.

You took me camping.

You really liked being a den mother.

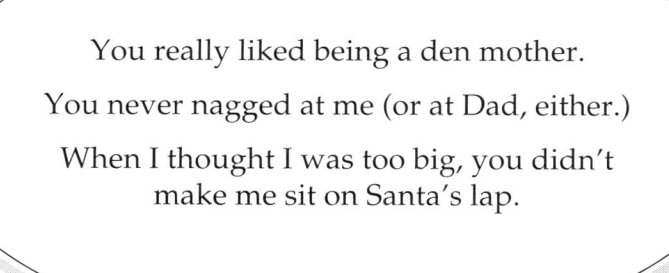

You never nagged at me (or at Dad, either.)

When I thought I was too big, you didn't make me sit on Santa's lap.

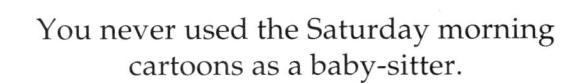

You never used the Saturday morning cartoons as a baby-sitter.

You let me stay up until midnight on New Year's Eve.

You made watching television a family activity.

You read the newspaper comics to me when I was too young to read them for myself.

If I asked you why, you always tried to give me an answer.

You admitted that you didn't know everything.

You taught me to cherish the family keepsakes, even if they weren't valuable in a monetary sense.

If I was interested in something, you took me to the library to find a book on the subject.

We learned things together.

You taught me never to close my mind to new ideas.

You took care of me.

You taught me to keep a file for important papers so I'd know exactly where they were when I needed them.

You let me help you knead the bread and make a little loaf for myself.

You let me teach you about computers and got an E-mail address so I could "talk" to you on-line.

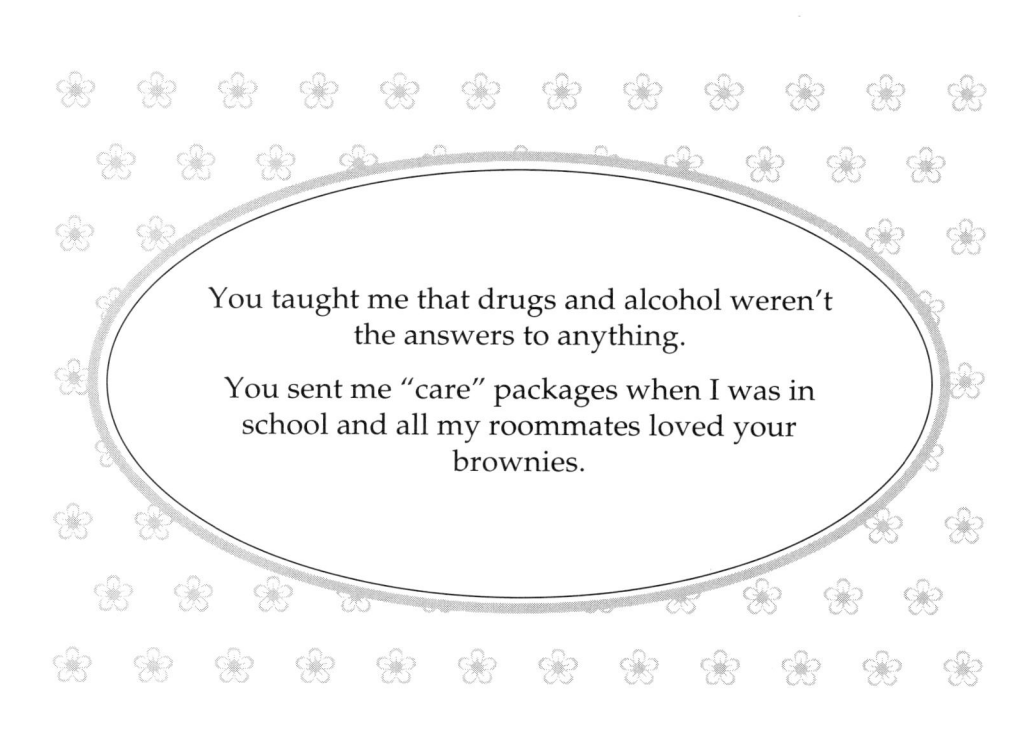

You taught me that drugs and alcohol weren't the answers to anything.

You sent me "care" packages when I was in school and all my roommates loved your brownies.

You answered my questions about sex honestly.

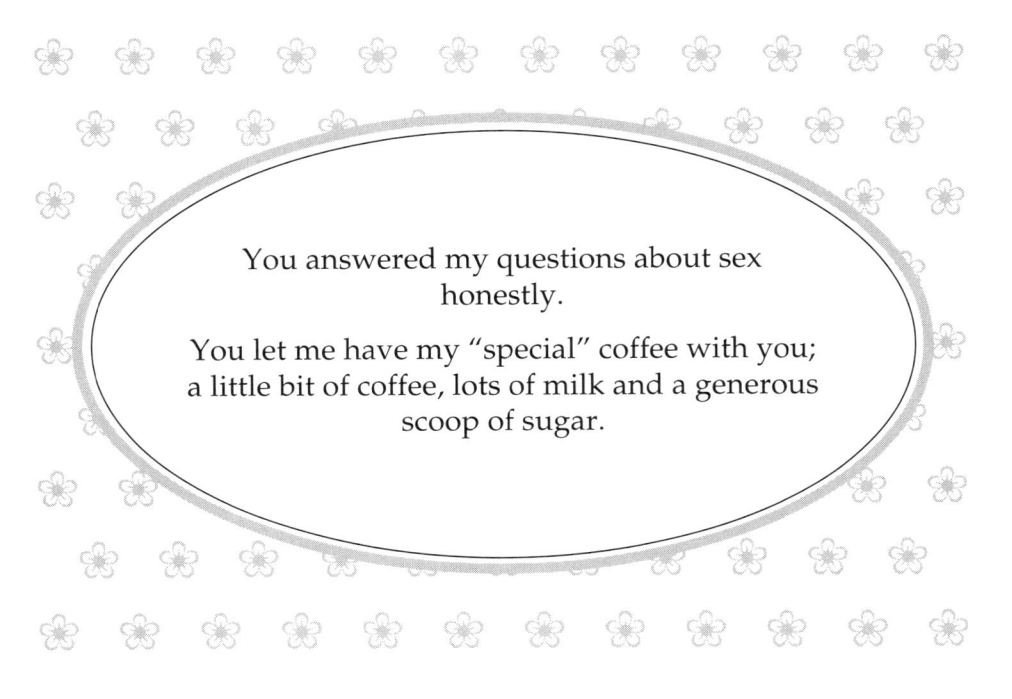

You let me have my "special" coffee with you; a little bit of coffee, lots of milk and a generous scoop of sugar.

You proved that it doesn't take a whole village
to raise a child, just one good mother.

You let me have a camp-out with my friends
in the backyard.

You helped me build a tree house and asked
Dad to test it to make sure it was safe.

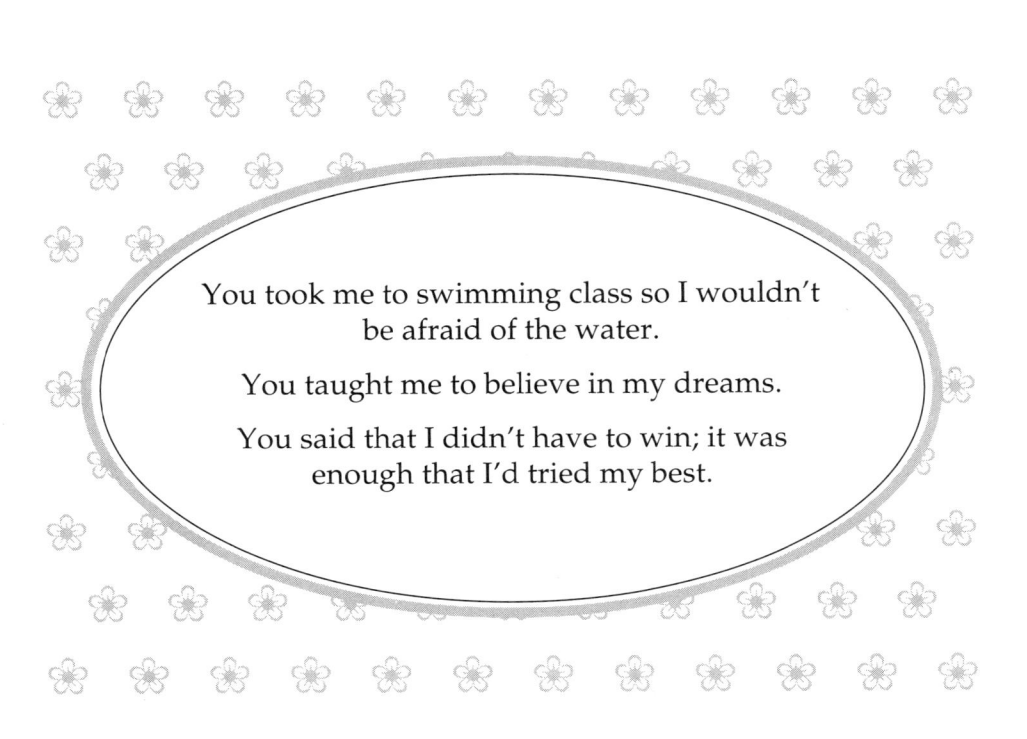

You took me to swimming class so I wouldn't be afraid of the water.

You taught me to believe in my dreams.

You said that I didn't have to win; it was enough that I'd tried my best.

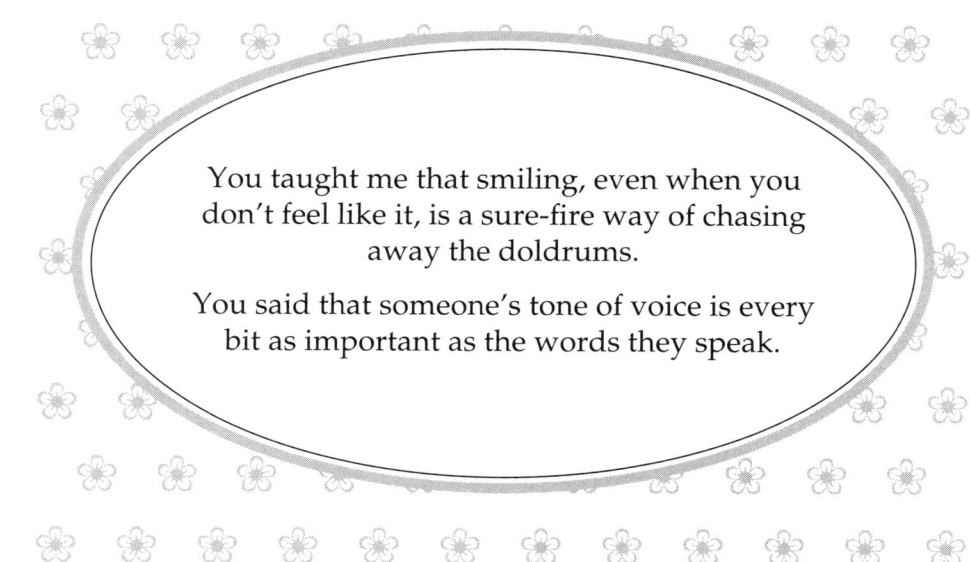

You taught me that smiling, even when you don't feel like it, is a sure-fire way of chasing away the doldrums.

You said that someone's tone of voice is every bit as important as the words they speak.

You told me stories about when you and Dad first met.

You taught me to look for the reasons why people do the things they do.

You never seemed to mind driving us places and picking us up.

You said that singing in the shower is an excellent way to start the day.

You made popcorn for us when we watched movies on television.

You said it was wise to withhold judgment until I was sure.

You said that all the money in the world won't buy love; it comes from the heart and is freely given.

You showed me that a homemade gift is much more precious than an expensive trinket from the store

When I did something foolish, you didn't get angry. You just asked me to explain exactly why I did it.

You gave me privacy when my friends came to visit, but you were always close by if I needed you.

You showed me how to enjoy the weather; the wonder of capturing a perfect snowflake on my hand, the feel of cool rain on my skin, the way the wind lifts my hair, and the comforting warmth of the summer sun.

You always accepted me the way I was.

You taught me to be a survivor.

You've given me a million reasons to be glad that you are my Mom.